THE NATIONAL POETRY SERIES

The National Poetry Series was established in 1978 to publish five books of poetry every year through participating trade publishers. Publication of the books is funded by James Michener, Edward J. Piszek, The Copernicus Society, The Witter Bynner Foundation for Poetry, Patricia Robinson, The Mobil Foundation, and the five publishers: Random House, Doubleday & Company, E. P. Dutton, Harper & Row, and Holt, Rinehart and Winston.

The National Poetry Series—1983

Joanne Kyger, *Going On: Selected Poems* (Selected by Robert Creeley)

Jane Miller, *The Greater Leisures* (Selected by Stanley Plumly)

Donald Revell, *From the Abandoned Cities* (Selected by C. K. Williams)

Susan Tichy, *The Hands in Exile* (Selected by Sandra McPherson)

John Yau, *Corpse and Mirror* (Selected by John Ashbery)

Corpse and Mirror

CORPSE AND MIRROR

JOHN YAU

HOLT,
RINEHART
AND
WINSTON

An Owl Book

NEW
YORK

Published by Holt, Rinehart and Winston,
383 Madison Avenue, New York, New York 10017.
Published simultaneously in Canada by Holt, Rinehart and
Winston of Canada, Limited.

Library of Congress Cataloging in Publication Data
Yau, John, 1950-
Corpse and mirror.
(The National poetry series)
Includes bibliographical references.
I. Title. II. Series.
PS3575.A9C6   1983   811'.54   82-15544
ISBN: 0-03-063041-X

First Edition

Designer: Joy Chu
Printed in the United States of America
1 3 5 7 9 10 8 6 4 2

"The Reading of an Ever-Changing Tale" first appeared in
The Reading of an Ever-Changing Tale (Nobodaddy Press, 1977);
"Chinese Villanelle," "The Lost Colony," "Nantucket," and
"Shimmering Pediment" first appeared in Sometimes (Sheep
Meadow Press, 1979); "Rumors," "Brief Item," "Shanghai
Shenanigans," "The Dream Life of a Coffin Factory in Lynn,
Massachusetts," and "Broken Off by the Music" first appeared in
Notarikon (Jordan Davies, 1981); "Late Night Movies" and
"Scenes from the Life of Boullée" first appeared in Broken Off by
the Music (Burning Deck, 1981).

These poems appeared originally in the following publications:
The Black Warrior Review: "The Pleasures of Exile"; Low Tech
Manual: "Two Kinds of Song"; Meadline: "Aztec Love Song";
Sulphur: "Carp and Goldfish"; Boxcar: "Corpse and Mirror I,"
"Corpse and Mirror II," and "Corpse and Mirror III"; Sun:
"January 18, 1979" (under the title "Winter Moment"); Bridge:
"After the War (I–IV)."

Acknowledgment is made to Alfred A. Knopf, Inc., for permission
to quote from The Demons by Heimito Von Doderer, translated by
Richard and Clara Winston. Copyright © 1961 by
Alfred A. Knopf, Inc.

FOR WILLIAM AND BEVERLY CORBETT

And yet—in fact you need only draw a single thread at any point you choose out of the fabric of life and the run will make a pathway across the whole, and down under that pathway each one of the other threads will become successively visible, one by one. For the whole is contained in the smallest segment of anyone's life-story; indeed, we may even say that it is contained in every single moment; start up your dredging machine and you will take it all up, no matter whether ecstasy, despair, boredom, or triumph happens to fill the remaining buckets on their endless chain of ticking seconds.

—Heimito Von Doderer
The Demons

CONTENTS

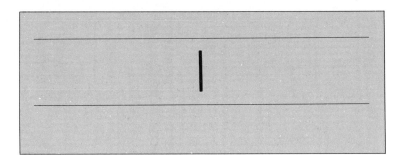

I

PARALLEL
LIVES

Parallel Lives

Bowing sweetly beneath the crystal chandelier
Is the poet and architect of gardens,
Alexander Pope. Directly across from him
Is the amply proportioned Lady Wednesday,
Who, I might add, has just arrived
In the guise of a postcard
Depicting a grim-faced Aztec deity bent beneath
A disc meant to represent the sun.

Carillons inform us that it is late
In the afternoon; and in this diminishing light
Lady Wednesday finds it impossible
To recall her recent past, a world
Where each day is as unique
As the man-like god, whose only task
Is to protect and deliver the sun
To its underground chamber.

Alexander Pope, on the other hand,
Designed a tunnel leading from his house
To the walled garden across the street.
How he hated to hobble across that street,
Or any street in the bright corrosive sunlight.
How always people muffled their amazement
At the deformed body he carried
Everywhere, like a lazy brother.

In the furnace-like universe
The Aztecs inherited, there were
Neither jokes nor aphorisms to exchange.
Alexander Pope was different.
He could laugh at everyone,
But himself. It was the difference
Of disease that made him bitter.

In his childhood he had had polio,
And the memory of it grew out of his back
Until he resembled a squat reptile.
Darting tongue, flickering eyes,
He lived long enough to write his poems,
While the Aztec god's life lasted a day—
Exactly the length of his task.

But now—as evening drops
Its newspaper onto the porch—
I must leave them
Just as I found them, dancing;
Joined together in their deformity,
And the need to deliver something
To its correct destination,
Its intended recipient.

Rumors

At the beginning of a street some say never ends
is a statue whose inscription says otherwise.

Some rivers remain questions, shifting
from side to side. Other questions
remain rivers, thick and muddy.
One bridge is a moth-eaten highway.
Another is a rhinestone bridge.

An architect wants to build a house
rivaling the mountains surrounding
his sleep, each turret mute as a hat.
He crosses a river to reach ground
hard enough to begin his plan. He crosses
a river the way a river crosses his sleep,
swirling with questions.

The inscription says the river flows back
into the mountain carrying the dead.
Silver coins on their eyes. Silver coins
engraved with the faces of those left behind.
On squealing streets. On pavements
rippling beneath a pyramid of glances.

At the beginning of a street some say never ends
is a river curving beneath the city, carrying
the architect to sleep. Every morning
the clouds resemble something more terrifying,
until all resemblance ends, and he wakes up
in an empty hall, alone on a river.

For Alexander Pope's Garden

In a garden every plant and flower
Memorizes the proper manner
In which to behave, or else they are discarded.
The lessons are simple; the growth must be retarded
Until they stand like dragoons in an orderly row,
Keep their thoughts private, and occasionally bow.

Two Kinds of Song

It is said the palace was modeled on a dream, but even what the king remembers of his dream is not necessarily the dream itself. Will this space between the pages of sleep and the writing of day always exist? I do not know. I might never know. I am only a guard—a fixture that moves like the polished hands of a clock.

It is said there is nothing about your life the king does not know. All of the halls surrounding his private chambers are painted blue to remind us how the sky, where he and the gods converse nightly, lies forever beyond our reach. Today, from the tower, I watched the clouds scurrying overhead. They were in a tizzy, almost like newlyweds shopping for dinner in the marketplace. Maybe the priests are right. Maybe the king does know what I am thinking, for even my metaphors defeat me.

Now, the only glimpse of hope I have is when I am assigned to the corridor where stately rows of deities smile at me from their dusty niches. When I am near them I feel something is askew, that the dream was remembered incorrectly, and these statues, these material echoes of the invisible, know more than they are saying, even to the king. And, at dawn, as I return to the barracks to sleep, I hear the birds singing in the emperor's garden, singing as if their song was meant only for the deaf.

II

CORPSE AND MIRROR

Corpse and Mirror (I)

1

When one of our citizens dies, his corpse is placed in his chariot. To help him reach his destination, his favorite horses are buried with him.

By the time dawn breaks out of its cage in the mountains, the gravediggers have gently lowered the chariot and its contents into a pit. Now, the horses must be rounded up and measured with the precision of a tailor. For each of these nervous engines must fit smoothly into its own grave, so only the head with its fearful yet fiery eyes emerges above the ground, like a hand rising from the sea.

Once the gravediggers have accomplished this task, they return immediately to the city. Their pace is quickened by the knowledge that inside their kitchens steam has started rising from glistening slabs of meat, tureens of brightly colored vegetables, and baskets of earth-colored breads.

All afternoon they have dreamed of entering a room like this, full of solace and celebration. And yet, when each of them reaches its door, they hesitate; almost as if they wished they could join the procession of heads towing an invisible cargo toward the setting sun, the next city that must be reached before dawn escapes once more.

If the man's sins outweigh his acts of kindness, the horses will eventually collapse and blood will stream from their nostrils. Beneath the moon the man will revive, but he will have become so hideously ugly since his last breath left him that no one—not even the most generous of samaritans—will be able to offer him food and shelter. He will remain in this condition, doomed to wander in the desert like a vulture without wings.

The only way he will be given another chance is if one of his neighbors dreams about him in the week following his death. In the dream the man must give his exact location beneath the stars. At dawn, the neighbor must ride out to the spot and see if he is there. If he isn't, the kindhearted neighbor must dismount at once and begin praying, for he has been deceived once again. Death has not prevented the deceased from continuing along the path he chose in life. If the neighbor does not pray at once, he must give up all hope of ever finding his way back to the city. The dead man has chosen him for a companion, and he has been foolish enough to accept.

When one of our citizens dies, his head is cut off and placed inside a mirror-lined box. The box is tightly sealed, allowing no light to enter its interior, and placed inside the least used room of the house. Each night, someone from the family must sleep beside the varnished cube in which the head resides. After two weeks have elapsed, the box can be buried beside the rest of the corpse.

However, if everyone in the family bears a grudge against the deceased, an anger so deep that death has not removed its poison, they may burn the box and joyfully kick the ashes and bone fragments into the river. The decision must be reached without ever being mentioned. Finally, once the ashes begin floating downstream, the deceased's name can never be brought up in conversation again.

Once the head is inside the box, the eyelids will push against the weight of dreams and sleep until they open. It will never occur to him that his head has been severed from his body. Instead, he will believe he has been kidnapped and buried in the sand. Before him is a road stretching to the horizon. Above him the moon patrols the walls of its vast domain. Escape is impossible. By morning the vultures will begin circling patiently.

Soon he begins rambling, imagining his mouth is parched and full of sand. This is a signal. Whoever is sleeping in the room must awaken immediately and begin listening to the voice echoing inside the box. What happens next depends on who has died. If instructions are uttered, they must be followed faithfully. If a confession is made, it must be heard without judgment. Whatever is said must be kept a secret.

If you are sent to another city, you must saddle your horse at dawn and leave without speaking to anyone. Once you are there, you must find the house the voice described. A house similar to all the houses on all the winding streets in this haphazardly designed city, and yet different in one essential way. When the door opens you will know why. However, if the person who answers the door is puzzled by your request, then you have failed to listen to the instructions carefully enough. Too many words slipped through your excitement. In this case, you must return to your house without speaking to anyone along the way. No one in your family will greet you. You cannot sleep beside the box again, but must remain inside your room until the two weeks are over.

One night, after the box has been buried or burned, you will hear something outside your window, inside your dream. The words may not be words at all, but the fluttering of a bird caught in a snare. A broken pot. A bucket falling into a well. Listen carefully. He may need to speak to you once again.

Brief Item

Someone is hacking someone apart in a city
whose name rhymes with your own; a city you
never heard of before; a city you cannot visit
even though it visits you the way the day begins;
the way the day begins with a shimmering pulse
a pulse of expectation followed by a need
to hear someone call your name.

Corpse and Mirror (II)

1

When a comet passes over the town, whoever sees it knows a corpse will be discovered at the edge of the forest shortly after dawn.

Last week, an old woman who embroiders tablecloths with human hair saw one from her kitchen window, and knew her grandson had wandered too far from the road leading home.

Now, whenever she stops to talk to someone, she asks them whether the message was delivered too early or remembered too late.

If they are lying faceup with their eyes open and clear, as if they are still puzzled by the last thing they saw, then they must be cremated, their ashes scattered over the lake.

If, however, they are lying facedown with their eyes closed, as if they had dozed off while recalling the intricate lattice of a pleasant hour they passed through years ago, then they must be buried at once. No stone can mark the spot.

Otherwise, both the deceased and its discoverer are doomed to remember a moment, its sunlit basket of fruit, as if each drop of significance will forever elude them.

Some find it impossible to believe their life is chained to a comet. If they were to submit to the possibility the stars have exiled us from their provinces, then they would have to accept that the story unfolds without them.

In the afternoon you see them huddled in the corners of dark cafés. Sometimes, their mumbling reaches the street the way the sound of dry branches rubbing against each other pierces a dream.

Then one is awakened by a comet passing overhead; and once again the light echoing in our eyes reminds us that we were meant to wander from one day to the next, like dogs without masters.

2

When you break a mirror, you must count up the pieces to see if they add up to your age. If they do, you must change your name and leave town at once.

Do not speak to anyone you meet on the road until you have reached a town, where everyone speaks a language different from your own. Otherwise, you will wake up in someone else's coffin.

Do not tell anyone your name until you have forgotten every affectionate endearment you were summoned by as a child. Otherwise, one morning, the only voice you hear will be your own, echoing down the long hallways beneath sleep.

The voice will begin telling you a story about a child who hears someone calling his name. No matter which way the child turned, the source of the voice eluded him. And, as the story enters daylight's tenement, you will realize that you are the child, and it is your voice calling.

Persons in the Presence
of a Metamorphosis

The porcelain bayonet of noon scrapes the face
of a man who has forgotten why he started
to spit. A uniformed girl,

tiny and tireless, memorizes words
she believes make accurate mirrors.
A nun felt damp and gray,

like the windows of a plumber.
The porcelain glaze of noon filtering in
through the windows felt damp and gray,

like the unshaven face of a man
who has forgotten why he started to drink.
A uniformed girl trips, scrapes her knee,

and spits out a word she learned in class
when the nun left the room
to find a Bible with none of its pages missing.

A plumber cleans and polishes a bayonet
even though he believes they make lousy mirrors.
Devotion guides his hands;

eyes, tiny and tireless, like fish
swirling in their cloudy bowl.
In porcelain rooms a nun collects watches,

a uniformed girl polishes bayonets,
and a plumber looks for a word
with none of its pages missing.

Corpse and Mirror (III)

1

When the movie ends and the lights come on, the audience is puzzled by the sight of a corpse reclining on a velvet sofa in clothes of human hair. Each item has been carefully sewn, so that the hair resembles a white silk shirt and a three-piece wool suit flecked with gold.

On the mahogany table is a brass ashtray in the shape of a bulldog. Smoke curls from its nostrils as if it had swallowed a cigarette. An emerald butterfly glistens on his left index finger. In his bluish gray hands is a book whose pages are made of glass.

The next afternoon I drive to the outskirts of town, where there is a restaurant named after a traitor famous for his ingenious disguises. Many of its patrons think that even the name is a disguise and he still moves among us.

I have never been able to remember the plot of the movie, only the colors it traced against the arch of the bridge connecting the room's two halves together. On one side shines the movie and on the other sits the corpse. Passing back and forth between them is a conversation made of human hair.

2

When the movie ends, the lights come on. The audience is puzzled by the sight of a large oval mirror leaning awkwardly against a column, which wasn't there at the beginning of the evening's entertainment.

Scarves stop fluttering; and, one by one, hands settle nervously into laps, like birds circling the perimeters of their nests. Mouths twist beneath the receding wave of whispers, almost as if there were a place they could hide.

A reflection pierces the mirror, though the stage is empty. The men see a woman brushing her hair, while the women see a man trimming his beard.

Later, no one will be able to agree on what they saw. The memory of one event will twist around the memory of another. All that remains is the ache of trying to recall a moment, whose slanting roof of sunlight has long since fallen in. By then the mirror will have vanished and the movie will have started. This time in pieces.

Late Night Movies

In a small underground laboratory the brain of a
movie actor is replaced by semiprecious stones,
each one thought to have once resided in heaven.

An archaeologist realized the inside of an ancient
mask carried a picture of satin meant only for its
dead inhabitant. A nurse walked into a hospital
and knew something was missing.

In the afternoon, rain washed away all traces
of the railroad station. A crow hid its head
under its wing. A tourist sneezed twice and
wondered if there was any truth to the legend
inscribed over the doorway of the pharmacy.

Beware the opinions of a dead movie actor,
an empty hospital and a wounded crow on a rainy afternoon,
a missing brain and a train station built beside a river,
a nurse carrying a photograph of heaven.

In a small laboratory in heaven the semiprecious
thoughts of a movie actor are replaced by a brain.
The ancient mask realized the insides of the
archaeologist exuded a tincture of *Pisa*
meant only for its dead inhabitant.

Outside the train station the nurse wondered if
there was any truth to the legend inscribed
around the rims of her new tires. The brain
of the movie actor is carried by a tourist
from one day to the next.

In a small underground temple the wing of a crow
is replaced by semiprecious stones, each one
thought to have been a sneeze from heaven.

The nurse hid the hands of Orpheus under a painting
of a train station, whose shadows reached the river
where all legends began. A doctor realized the
doorway of the pharmacy was missing. A woman
wondered why a picture of heaven had replaced
her tires.

The movie actor's only desire was to be seen
by the dead, to be fixed in the lining
of clouds over their graves.

The archaeologist slept in a hospital with
as many windows as days in a year, and wondered
if there was any truth to the legend inscribed
on the semiprecious stones the tourist carried
across the plaza in the afternoon rain.
At times, the nurse thought the only desires
were the ones without names.

The head of Orpheus floated downriver, leaving
behind the hospital, where, as one version
of the legend claimed, the song would continue
forever in the hallways leading to the sea.

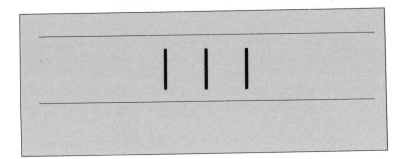

III

VARIATIONS ON CORPSE AND MIRROR

Variation on Corpse and Mirror

When a corpse meets a corpse there is a mirror between them.

Hours before the game is scheduled to start the arena is packed. Arriving from the east with the necessary backdrop is the sky, speckled with clouds, and carrying a pale yellow sun. Pennants wag their blue and green tongues. Rows of amulets bob up and down.

A few of the centaurs guffaw and stamp their hooves. Others are content to whisper quietly about the possible combinations. Bets are made between friends and among rivals. Conversations start and end with money, while, here and there, an empty cup (sign of impatience) floats down from the upper tiers, littering an otherwise empty field.

Short white hair, turquoise dress. She stands at the bus stop, aware she has forgotten to bring the flowers. By now the sun is shuffling its yellow cards beside the note left on the counter.

In the restaurant surrounded by alligators munching their way through another evening of entertainment. In the next room someone turns the page, and laughs.

Sunlight flopped over the windowsills facing the sea. In another room in another house in another city tears are labeled according to consistency and circumstance.

She quashes an apparent need to moan, perhaps scream, and chooses instead a soft sigh meant to attract attention without eliciting a response. In the next room someone shuffles money, and laughs.

Once, in a month of blue moons, they slept in Siena, while people ran through the streets, screaming. Feverish with the news or news of the fever?

During the night legions of centaurs had amassed on the hills overlooking the city. By noon their guns gleamed like teeth, but their teeth still chattered. Matted fur of an army that marched for days in the rain.

The smell burns the nostrils for weeks. The piles of hacked and twisted limbs mounting at every streetcorner. They begin staying in their room. They begin talking as if the past is all they have to look forward to.

He imagines she wears a short white dress, has flowing turquoise hair. Often they dance beneath the chandelier of stars. Or beneath the bandages a face hidden behind a face.

Satisfied everyone could see what they had paid to witness, the architect left the stadium without noticing the clouds circling the sun. Or without cornices, arches, and pillars, masons constructed the arena near the center of the city. Vacant eyesocket pierced by centuries of sunlight and rain, the twin javelins elected to guard the city.

I left the stadium when the outcome was no longer in doubt. Birds were struggling to form a red necklace above the rooftops. Later, I saw waves leapfrogging in the harbor, stone after stone sliding into place, until a boat tilted precariously among the pyramids of ice.

From his seat he watches, hears himself whisper, fear etching its imprint into the tunnel burrowing through his voice. Often she turned, and turned away. Slender neck above a white dress.

What she remembered most was the moon's cold and bitter wine.

That morning they stood at the bus stop, each wishing the other would mention what had happened to the flowers. Neither was able to start the conversation, but on the bus it became impossible to talk among a group of raucous students stamping their feet, waving black and yellow pennants.

Everything else happened shortly before noon. Shortly before I saw eggshells drifting across the plaza. By then the sounds had reached us; and we knew that outside the city someone had nailed a note into the sky, and someone else's forehead was bleeding.

Aztec Love Song

When the skin is flayed a voice emerges,
throat of a song you strangle only once

Only once the voice is decapitated the body
returns—vibrant flower on a cold windowsill

Windowsill of water; the clouds remain clouds
as I turn, remembering how an earlier moment—

moment of parts, part of a moment—dwindles
into a face whose contours are almost apparent

Almost apparent beneath today's slab of sky
a blue dish with egg yolk smeared across its horizon

Second Variation on Corpse and Mirror

The femur was broken when the body was flung through
the windshield and landed beneath the car.
Teeth broken, tongue cut.

Begin outside the body in the hall leading past
the room. When you learn to walk you will have to
start at the beginning. Memory going one way,
the body another. Something wedged in between.

Tonight the streets are surrounded by the same sentences add-
ing up to a gray door, window overlooking a newly built park-
ing lot, river hidden behind trees, and tears I never saw. The
Aztecs did not believe in accidents, and sent their children into
the forest at night to gather scorpions. If he did not return
with the others, it was not the parents' loss but the gods' gain.

The room contained two beds.

At times morphine was injected into the body,
causing the mind to imagine fire did not burn.

World balanced on the back of a turtle, or box in which someone
slept and woke and saw their mother winking back. Tonight,
the sentences add up to a street beside which you sit, sipping
tea and pointing to the stars. The room contained two beds.
Beside the window a woman speaking. North of this room is
another larger room. There, her child was kept inside a box,
machines pumping what the heart could not.

Begin outside the room, beneath the trees,
seated between the cars in the parking lot.
First time in nearly a year without a window
between you and the clouds.

The morning you found out what happened after you went to sleep, woke up surrounded by smoke. Someone's tears along with the letter. Tonight, reading about the shape of the altar where the heart was surgically removed. And then the envelope came, delivering what the machines could not.

Stories are windows,
so much hacked away.

Child in a box and nothing else possible
until the wedge obstructing the orderly procedures
of the heart is removed.

In front of the desk a window, glare of the streetlight reaching past where a cat howls, and trees sway in the shreds of what is left over from the day.

Missing Pages

From the balcony of the seaside hotel you can see the jeweled towers rising from the bay's seemingly calm waters. Some say they are the remnants of an ancient port, the survivors of an earthquake. But it seems unlikely such a rupture in the earth's mantle could leave these edifices behind, each of them as bright and unmarred as they were on the morning the masons and priests dismantled the scaffolding, and stood back to see what had been accomplished in obdurate stone.

By the second morning of our visit, these symbols of the miraculous are the axis around which all our routines revolve. Our meals are eaten on the balcony, or by the window when it rains. Inevitably, our walks end up at the edge of the pier. And, on the one morning they were shrouded in fog, we shuffled aimlessly through the hotel corridors, unable to do anything but commiserate with each other over their absence.

The one fact that saved us, of course, was the realization we were guests on this island. But for the people living here it must be different. Each of us has wondered why they do not question the presence of these towers glowing offshore on the nights the moon anchors its orange boat above the harbor. The band continues playing its repertoire of favorite tunes and the bartender tells the same stories about the woman who left him for his best friend's brother.

Evidently, they have a ritual that takes everything into account. This evening, at our farewell dinner, we were told that on the first warm day of spring a legend begins circulating among those sitting in the park. It is a great honor to be there, but it is not something one should seek too often. Initially, the legend discusses only the earliest history of the towers. The priest who received a dream from heaven and the queen who commanded a monument be built to her brave dead husband were stories used up long ago. Now, our host told us with a smile, the legend must begin elsewhere—not in dreams and memory, but in daylight and desire.

Anyone can add whatever they like to the story, or take some chunk of it away, if, in their opinion, it impedes the narrative flow. At the beginning of summer (or the tourist season) the story, by then refined into its smoothest chapters, is written down by the mayor. A vote is taken by the council. If it passes approval, which it always does after a few revisions are made, the story is sealed away in a vault.

In the fall, when school begins, the children of the island are taught the story in their classes. It becomes the basis for the entire curriculum; literature, mathematics, even biology and the other natural sciences. In this way the children learn what must be forgotten, if they are to continue sleeping in their whitewashed cottages by the sea.

Third Variation on
Corpse and Mirror

I crossed the street
but not before
noticing the knife
poised along the moment's
throat, ready to divide
its destination into
two further choices.
In the yard beside me
two dogs played catch
with someone's head,
while a hand waved good-bye
to the body it once carried.

The Pleasures of Exile

About an hour before dawn the women squeeze themselves into wicker chairs. Directly before each of them is a window overlooking the town square. All the windows have long since agreed on one thing; there is a fountain overflowing with dried black leaves and a stray dog snapping at the moonlight.

In just a few minutes the statue in front of the hospital will begin raising his sword ever so slightly, hoping to make the sun appear a moment or two sooner to the bedridden. Later, in the lengthening shadows of the blue afternoon, the sword will be lowered, as if the day had stayed long enough.

It is said that only he, with his medals and faraway gaze, can find the door the sun must take to reach the next village. No one knows if that village is like this one. No one has ever bothered to go there, though it lies just beyond the forest.

None of these stories interests the women sitting in front of their windows. They are too busy trying not to be fooled by the wind. From the way they are sitting, from the tilt of their heads, it is clear that they all agree on one thing; they want to hear the approaching footsteps of their husbands and sons, the shifting of loose stones on the gravel path.

If they hear them in the distance, they know their husbands and sons will soon enter the town square, quickly and efficiently. Then each of them will turn without ceremony toward the appropriate street, the correct door.

Finally, when the last man enters the last door, all the curtains are drawn. The engines of the sun are about to arrive. Day will start, while, nearby, the wind will stir in the meadow, a restless dreamer.

A few moments after dawn spills down the mountain, a bird begins carrying a pebble in his beak. Hour after hour the husbands and sons share in this task of circling a field, finding a pebble, soaring out over the bay.

Sometimes, I felt as if my wings were the arms of a man

rowing against the tide, my boat piled high with cargo.

Other times I am the pebble dropped again and again.

I know I shall wake up in the next village and be the shadow of the dog barking at the ribbon of moonlight swirling around and around his legs.

I stop and look up at the windows. They are listening intently to the wind roaming through the orchards. The first apple is beginning its descent.

All I know is that years from now, when its glistening torso rolls across these cobblestones, no children will come out to greet it.

IV

SCENES FROM THE LIFE OF BOULLÉE

FOR RAE BEROLZHEIMER

1

Roof shaped like a strawberry. Hurriedly torn
paper towel. The queen's staircase does not
lead to the king's chamber. The traditional
requirements of comfort and convenience.
A kind of sleepwalking echoed by a line
in history. Stands on a lovesick giant
and calls himself a hero. Sound of annoyance
at an unforeseen circumstance becoming an
inevitable consequence. Wine dripping off
the formica table onto the shag rug after
hitting the unused wooden chair covered
with cigarette burns. A dream heard
secondhand. An extra coat hanger.
Only half the story is true. The rest
is necessary, like clouds on a cloudy day.

2

Pieces of a piece. The face in the window larger
than the window facing in. A mermaid selling
cheese in a laundromat in Ottawa. A cop who looks
as if he has to go to the bathroom. A bony hand
dangling from a red station wagon. Riding in a cab
with a junkie who wants an alarm clock. Breaking
a promise and counting the pieces. Her harsh
lipstick crumbling over her harsher smile.
Remnants of a collision in a galaxy whose
name is a number. Eeriness of a city with
only one light. The kinds of certainty
available in a drugstore. Jumbo food.
With only one light on. A junkie dangling
from an alarm clock. Using the laundromat
because there were no bathrooms around.
Stealing the mermaid's cheese. Breaking
into her smile. The kinds of certainty
available in a supermarket, a newspaper,

a lover. A young cop who looks as if he
has gone. The square face in the round
window. Pieces of a blue piece.

3

Without noticing the fire descending into the
subway station. Descending into the copper
sunlight. Going back again and again.
Their voices. One dripping. The other dribbling
to a stop. Lengthening each of the sounds into
a staircase. I think there's three volumes.
A salmon. A sale's on. Ceylon. Existence
being the only record of their names.
Shoes seen by the side of the highway
leading to Las Vegas. Faces remembered
from last Thursday. Talking to an imaginary
friend in your sleep. Waking up and feeling
the sweat. The sweet surrounding your skin.
Adding to the pile. The only thing invisible
for miles. In every kind of light. The light
of topless dancing. Only half of you is there.
No music sparring with traffic. Enters
in a suit the color of coffee, face the color
of masking tape. Everyone looks like you, today.
Even people I don't like.

4

A room with open windows facing a street
where dogs gather at night. Falling curtain.
Refrigerator whose parts can't be replaced.
A full garbage bag waiting for someone by not
waiting for anything. Smoke on a horizon that
exists as a footnote. Unable to see all of
the sky all at once, how the city breaks it
into the pieces needed to cross the street.
Ridden speechless. Frogs frozen under the

curving black marble table. Nothing closer
than the next smile to break the back of
the king. Residential talons. An ashtray
full of rubber bands. Happy with his
gladiatorial entertainment. Happy
with the smoke blocking out the sun.
When a place becomes a person
whose place it is.

5

The rising cost of heart attacks. Different-
colored bricks in a brick wall. The milky
water caused by adding a lemon. The need
for secondhand pacemakers. A fantastic
throne of irresponsibility. Names being
their only existence. Smell of clean
laundry. Sound of ginger ale bubbling
inside a can. Sound of irresponsibility.
Smell of their names being the only
record of their existence. The need
for secondhand bricks. Piece of
yellowing scotch tape peeling off
the cabinet door. Largest incision
possible. Adding a roof.

6

Zebra-striped pillow. The restlessness
of the jungle in a bed of poses. Not
what he had in mind, but what he had.
The rising cost of platitudes. Why
these questions, these answers, these
beginnings whose endings sail off into
familiar clichés. Suburbs of Samarkand.
Roof shaped like a milk carton. Dormer
window whose mystery was never resolved.
You can't judge a library by its cover.

Broken by the sand, the slipping away
on a shore not bound by the water.

7

Realizing that any certainty is an old one.
The difference between their similarities.
On the back alleys of cities whose avenues
are lushly described adventures. False starts.
Gleam of a cabin cruiser at night in a new
and otherwise empty parking lot. The round
caution with which she danced. The kind of
precociousness found only in octogenarians.

8

So much of the proscenium burned
away by its own curving pride.
Broken by the law of averages.
Toward the moonlight slipping down
banyan leaves. Characterized
by an earlobe. Under the twitching
grin was an often neglected acumen.
The clouds act like clouds. Snuggling
weather. Like a rope dangling from
a tree, a site where there is
more conjecture than hard knowledge.

9

Rubbing her sable with long thoughtful
fingers. Skimming the curdles of the dream.
His eyes, dull and tired, like grape seeds.
Gravy stains from the previous tenant.
Motific clouds. A summer shaped like
a hot dog, and its rungs of sunlight.
Nails—no two bent the same way.

10

The stumbling blocks are realigned
until a dome appears. After the lake
loses its flag of nervousness. A
parlorlike garage full of bicycles
and unmuddy children. A lemonade-colored
star. Nodding to the famous twins
sitting in opposite windows. Crossing
the river while the sun is about to set
like a moustache on a windowsill. But
it is a happiness without pleasure.

11

The sheets dangling from the line,
smudged photographs of snow.
A rising cenotaph of moonlight.
Surrounded by photographs of prosperity.
Quivering as if the birds had just left.
Sound of ginger ale bubbling inside a
bottle. Undistinguished except by this
reminder, this hurricane in an apple tree.

12

A casual solitude that is beyond casualness.
The snow braids its crumbling ladders.
A smudge of her smile remained on his cheek.
Surely, the wind will reach us, someday,
when the curtains have been drawn back
into their folds. Is it like knowing that
a clock is always surrounded by time?
They took luck to mean an accident which
benefited them all. The island still
presents a number of problems, though none
of them is as overwhelming as the rain
trickling down the walls. Then I wake up
and begin driving.

13

Counting the times as if they added up.
A haze flattens the city into a blackboard
that needs washing. The grime remaining.
The grim remains. Leaning against an
attitude out of fear. The cane of
canes. Bearing dignified fronts,
proud of them as they are of well-behaved
children. After losing the lorgnettes
in the taxi, their second afternoon
together was as round as a teacup.
The sound of their shovels eroding
into doubt. Watched their daughter
crying in a field, while the sky
unfurled its glistening poncho.

14

Stuffing yourself into a blizzard.
The heavy brass knocker in the form
of a laugh. The passageway leading
from the living room to the study
became a memory of other possibilities.
Red piano keys of sunset.
On a motorcycle beside a wheel
larger than you. On one
corner of a porch were two
coffee cups full of rainwater
and dust. The rope that might
have once restrained a dog.
Counting her gray hairs in the
blue mirror of the polished linoleum.
A barbarian surprise reached the gates
of the kingdom. The light shifted among
the leaves, like a rat. Skirted the edge
of her smile. Another autobiography
sinking beneath its glittering reflections.

The sky hopes to find a new purpose, while
hints of snow left a stain on every collar.

15
The scotch-tape scars on the wall. Scared
as a gorilla in a parachute. The moon
might be right on schedule, but the play
is over. Especially as the night remains
at our side, like a finger held up to
the lips. The headlights form an echo
around their glistening chrome. In the
window of the burned-out drugstore.
In the lengthening shadows of
the strawberry-colored roof.

16
The certainty of being part of the atmosphere
is also an aspirin. The desire to listen to
the cement of emotions as opposed to its
bricks. The various formats of disgrace,
and their subheadings, were one way he
avoided going to the store. The world
of institutions beside the institutions
of the world. The bartered bride is an opera.
But the battered bride is not singing.
The perfection of greed as a sign of the times.

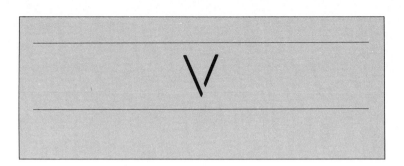

V

THE LOST COLONY

The Reading of
an Ever-Changing Tale

Certain colors got lodged under
the fingernails before their names
came to grace our speech. But
what of the phenomena whose
colors can only be imagined?
What did you do with the pills?
And why were you without any gasoline?
Today, these questions are a restraint
on your memory as the color
"blue" is a box opened up
like a sky under which
no grass grows. But traces remain.
The war you only just heard about
inextricably mixed with a face
you will probably never see again.

January 18, 1979

So often artists have painted a woman
washing, or combing her hair.
And nearby is a mirror.
And there you were, crouched in the tub.
It was cold in the apartment.
It is always cold in winter.
But you were brushing out your hair
and singing to yourself.
And, for a moment, I think I saw
what those artists saw—
someone half in love with herself
and half in love with the world.

Chinese Villanelle

I have been with you, and I have thought of you
Once the air was dry and drenched with light
I was like a lute filling the room with description

We watched glum clouds reject their shape
We dawdled near a fountain, and listened
I have been with you, and thought of you

Like a river worthy of its gown
And like a mountain worthy of its insolence
Why am I like a lute? left with only description

How does one cut an axe handle with an axe?
What shall I do to tell you all my thoughts
When I have been with you, and thought of you

A pelican sits on the dam, while a duck
Folds its wings again; the song does not melt
I remember you looking at me without description

Perhaps a king's business is never finished,
Though "Perhaps" implies a different beginning
I have been with you, and I have thought of you
Now I am like a lute filled with this wandering description

Three Poems for Li Shang-yin

1
When she left she took everything—her hair
Was a dream filled with colors gone by noon.
Yet, if nothing can be retrieved, I am still pulled
Toward this woman, who is still asleep, locked
Away in another life; her hair
Piled up like red peonies at noon.

2

No trace of you in the dust.
No footprints leading away from the house.
All morning I have been walking in this house,
For I am like a pile of dust
Shifting restlessly from room to room.
If you had been a shadow passing through my house,
You would have left nothing behind, not even dust.

3
The clouds change, but my dreams
Of you are always the same.
I see you walking and I call out—
Is it true? I ask, that if you
Dream of your lover, you
Can be assured he has deceived you.
And always your answer is the same.
How can I tell you? if the only place
We can meet, now, is in these dreams.

Shanghai Shenanigans

The moon empties its cigarette over a row of clouds
whose windowsills tremble in the breeze

The breeze pushed my boat through a series
of telephone conversations started by perfume

Perfume splashed over the words of a nomad
who believed it was better to starve than to laugh

To laugh over the administration's most recent mishap
will make the guests stay until the party

Until the party is bundled in chatter
I will count the pearls lingering around your neck

Any Day Now
You Will Return

Each time your phone rings
I start remembering
the simplest details.
On the roof of
a nearby building
a sunburned man feeds
his brood of prize pigeons.
In the afternoon
he watches them
circling above his head.
Outside Florence, Leonardo
observed a wheel spinning
in a bright blue rut of air.
On the wheel the Romans saw
was a glimpse of what
was about to arrive.
Chaldeans consulted dogs and flies.
The coffee is cold—
a film of milk covers it,
like a leaf. Two postcards
beside the cup.
The son of the wind
was once a man.
When he stands on his feet
it is quiet and still.
Today he is standing.
A hammock of birds
sways beneath the sun.
Each time I dial your phone
I think of the pigeons
rising from the roof—
the calm yet intent
flurry of their wings.

The Lost Colony

You were walking
down the street
and I almost called out your name.
A moment later I knew
it is all I would have done
because it is all I know of you, now.
Often we ask ourselves questions
we think will help.
They seldom do.
I was on my way to the store
to buy milk from Ramon,
who always tells me
what the weather is like.
I know it will happen again.
Both of us live on the narrow
part of this island.
Even the streets are narrow,
pressed up close together
like the buildings, though
neither is particularly intimate.
If anything, they are like
the rafts of clouds
scudding above us today
in that they are both
alike and unique.

After two years
and storms that forced him
back to England, Captain White
anchored off North Carolina's sandy coast.
How the clouds appeared to him
that morning might have meant
something different later.
The colonists he left behind were gone.

After searching the island,
the abandoned cabins
and untilled fields,
Captain White and his crew
find only a word carved on a tree.

Off to the Side

We were on opposite sides
of the street when we
saw each other and waved.
An instant where our reflexes
performed the polite form
from within our coats and gloves.
It was a brittle, dwindling
afternoon, almost as plain
as the words describing it.
You were saying good-bye
to a friend and I
was walking to the subway.
When you caught up
with me, we didn't turn,
for this time there was
no one there to see us.
Nor did we look
into the store windows—
their gray reflections
would contain us both,
and we only wanted to see
the other and not be seen.
Giotto often shows us
the back of someone's head.
It is a simple, effective device
telling us the drama
is occurring elsewhere.
For a moment we kept pace
(What else could we do?)
within the strictness
of the city, the numbers
on the doors following a logic
we believe in, if we are to reach

our destination still believing
parallel lines never meet.
And then that moment dissolved
and we were gone.

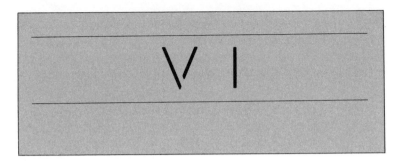

VI

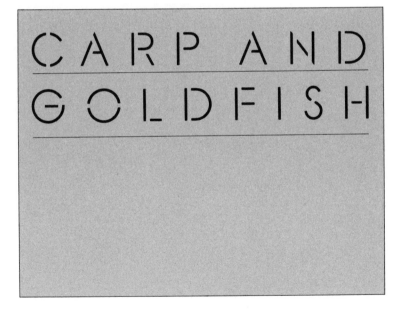

CARP AND GOLDFISH

Two Meditations on Guanajuato

1

Postcards are fragments of an encyclopedia; and typical of one announcing a town whose existence concerns only its tenacious inhabitants, this one's a photograph of the main attraction. San Antonio has its fort, Lugano its lake. But for those stopping in Guanajuato to take in the sights, the main attraction seems to be a little graveyard museum. The treasures lining its walls are some former citizens, all recently deceased. For the photograph seven mummies have been carefully posed: three adults and four infants.

On the back is written: "Well, yes, there are mummies in Guanajuato—they dig you up after five years in the crowded graveyard, but this is wonderful dry climate and preserves bodies—some of them—and the lucky ones get stood up in a hallway of some kind of graveyard museum—there's even a lady died during Caesarean operation and the kid on the umbilical cord with her. But I think the reason they won't decay is that they like their beautiful town so much they can't leave it."

At first glance they look like neighbors posing for a photograph taken at a suburban Halloween party. The adults have been propped up on a ledge about two feet off the floor. The woman has been placed between the two men. And, unlike her escorts, she is still in her coffin, which resembles a doorway to a tiny vestibule and has a pointed arch. It must be sunny and warm outside, for she is wearing what was once a white linen dress. Her arms are casually folded, as she has only stopped by for a moment to relay what she has just learned about the butcher and his long-nosed wife.

Both her escorts are nearly lost in their ill-fitting three-piece suits. A pocket watch dangles from the vest of the man on the left. Is one of the curator's duties to wind the watch every morning?

The baggy suits and dress reveal one aspect of the geology. If you are buried in the soil of Guanajuato, you shrink. Everything is squeezed out of you, like a sponge, until only the essential elements remain.

The man on the left is clutching his chest with both hands in obvious hysteria. His mouth is agape, his face contorted. Has he just realized he has lost his wallet and cannot pay the bill? Has he only just this minute consulted his watch and seen what time it is? Or was it simply he was buried alive? And his mouth is permanently open in the belief someday his screams would finally reach us.

The man on the right, shoulders stooped under an invisible weight, appears to be the most uncomfortable of the three. His arms dangle uselessly at his sides and his head is turned slightly toward the woman. He has been listening to her for a long time—longer than even he can remember—and knows it is not the same as paying attention to a cab driver who complains about what his wife fixed him for breakfast.

At the bottom of the woman's coffin is a child dressed in red, its head bowed and solemn. Were they buried together? And why?

The other children are dawdling on the floor. If anything, they are a ragged band of devoted cherubs. Like the angels, their sex is unclear, for they are all wearing the same kind of loose-fitting smock one sees in a hospital.

Despite the comic overtones of their narrative, everyone in the postcard radiates a persona of dignified homeliness. This condition is intensified by its irrevocability, as well as by the woman's ceaseless blathering, the man's permanent discomfort, and the realization the bill can never be rendered in full. And yet, for all their endless troubles, they seem genuinely relaxed, now that they are on eternal vacation from the inescapable poverty of Guanajuato.

There is something familiar about the way this collection of corpses is huddled in front of the camera, the way men are attending to a woman's needs. Their iconographic counterparts can be discovered in Masaccio's panel, *Madonna and Child with Saints*. In the painting everyone is stiff, homely, and graceful. Many scholars believe the deliberate stiffness of the Christ Child's pose foretells the rigidity of his death.

Not only do the bodies in the postcard bear a similar pose to those in Masaccio's panel, but there is also a corresponding stiffness to the way their gestures have affected their clothes, whether they are suits or robes, gown or a dress. In the postcard the clothes have succumbed to the same *rigor mortis* that invaded its inhabitants. And, as with the painting, an oddly natural light exhales throughout.

Clearly, Masaccio and whoever posed the mummies share an iconography, despite a time lapse of more than five hundred years. The only difference is in the moment; the painting depicts an event whose outcome is already known, while the postcard records what happens after the inevitability has occurred.

The idea of being able to dig someone up after five years and place their corpse in a museum is a rather grimly comical notion. Our ideas about death are more pristine. We want it clean, the grounds of the cemetery mowed. We do not want flies buzzing around our heads. And we certainly do not want row after row of gaping leers around to remind us that they might have had the last laugh. Even the names we give our cemeteries suggest the possibility of peace on earth. And yet, I am fascinated by this postcard; and I know if I ever go to Mexico, I will stop in Guanajuato and pay a visit to the inhabitants of its dusty museum.

2

I do not imagine anyone I know, including myself, would like to see their relatives propped up in the hallway of a local museum. Nor can I imagine many people I know would like to see their mother, sister, or wife associated with the Madonna in this fashion. In fact, that much maligned creature, the tour guide and his memorized spiel, is easier to imagine.

"That one over there is my ugly nephew, but this one is my beautiful, darling cousin." We would stop in the hallway and watch him, as he turned to us and continued lamenting the unfairness of fate to grant her such a short, hard life. An existence sucked out of her by the sun and soil itself, until all that remained of her was what we saw before us: a young, wizened girl in tatters.

When we finally reached the exit, he would remind us once again of the holes in her cotton dress, while each of us fumbled for change, knowing he would spend it later that evening in a bar. We might even return the following day to see if he chose another resident, changed his story. But more than likely we would continue our journey through Mexico, knowing whatever he said the second time would not remove the memory of what we first saw.

Isn't my urge to visit Guanajuato similar to the one I have when I go to the book store and buy an autobiography or biography? I want to know something more about someone? It is the only reason I look at photographs; Guanajuato's museum, for example. So why do I read autobiographies if I am unwilling to write one? It grows more complicated. For the postcard has become increasingly entangled with the idea of Christmas, my memories of it. And if the connection has remained constant yet vague—which it has—comical yet dull and unspecified, like a restless ache, then I must make it clear, at least to myself, if I am to get on with my daily activities.

In fact, I no longer need the postcard to prompt my memory. For months I have seen their wrinkled faces peering out of everyone I know. Their taut smiles, barely controlled hysteria, and relentless discomfort debut when least expected. I am unable to think of Christmas without remembering Guanajuato. They are like Siamese twins, one unable to breathe without the other. I know I must understand why they seem permanently joined. Otherwise, I am stuck, forever repeating their image in my mind, seeing their contorted faces while listening to a friend convey an anecdote.

Nothing seems to remove this distraction. And yet, if I am going to dig up the recent past and place it in a museum, if I am going to endow its banality with meaning, as anyone who writes about themselves does, I want it done quickly and efficiently, like the men who push their spades into the warm soil of Guanajuato. For it will be a museum I have no desire to visit. Arranging it will be enough.

The Dream Life of a Coffin Factory
in Lynn, Massachusetts

Earlier in the century it was not unusual to spend
an evening on the veranda. It was a time when
movie theaters sprawled around newly constructed
lagoons, their blue concrete walls rising out of
Wisconsin snowdrifts, their tile roofs fiercely
gathering Delaware's windswept soot in March.

Every street personalized its drugstore with
mahogany stools on which one could perch
and wait for evening to unfold its newspaper,
shake out its umbrella. And at night, long
after everyone was asleep, the rows of
chrome spigots still glistened with pride.

Now it was dusk; and floating above these
warm suburbs was a tremendous dome, whose
perimeter was molded with high-relief figures
of motorcycles and pouting dancers, wagon wheels
and other things classical.

In Wisconsin's lagoons it was still considered
graceful for a man to sit in a drugstore
and wait for a hand to squeeze an orange pill.

In Delaware's soot a woman could sit on a wall
and lose hours counting clouds unfolding in
the darkness.

It was, if anything, a newly constructed century—
a time when only motorcycles sprawled fiercely
in the rain.

Behind the movie theater a warm glow spread out
from the window of the hacienda, bravely gathering
the remnants of evening to its yellow handkerchief.

Even the narrower streets had their own lagoons,
each one lined with stucco clouds on which
one could sleep, waiting for evening to deliver
its pastel uniforms. It would remain an evening
of waiting, for men and women floated above
the suburbs, pouting fiercely
in the last stages of a withered century.

In March, in Wisconsin, young men shed their moustaches.
After carefully weighing them, they were placed in
linen handkerchiefs and buried in the snow. In the
evening they ran back to the classical suburbs, where
rows of young women leaned in glistening drugstores,
waiting for the clouds to get older.

The perimeter of these suburbs was carefully outlined
by chrome spigots. Lawns rose fiercely out of the snow,
while paper bags seldom crossed the avenue. If a newspaper
floated past a window, a pale hand clutched a withered foot.
It was a time when the century had gone to sleep,
and everyone glistened with pride.

Two Kinds of Story-Telling

1

Her childhood was composed of fairy tales. The places she described existed in a world accessible only to the words: "Once upon a time." China was a kind of Eden she could never return to, and he would never know, except by hearsay.

Clouds wrapped in silver foil.

A door whose room stretches down halls pointing to the sea.

A city whose walls curve out to meet lost travelers.

He wondered why they had fallen from grace, why they had been banished. It was not that her stories did not tell. It was that no answer could be found among the words. Nor was there any point to these stories. At least no moral point.

She talked about her childhood because she had to tell someone, and she thought no one but her son would listen, no one but her husband would know she was telling the truth.

2

People who think they are no longer imprisoned by their poverty always try to glamorize the past. What was awful about the past is mentioned only to reveal how the present is better, and how the future will be better still. Such stories are symbolic narratives incorporating the idea of change. The inspiration behind them is the passage of the *Mayflower* to the New World.

Her stories begin fitting into this genre after she has lived in America for a few years. At different points in her life she attempts to write them down. They will be about the moment her life changed. They will be about why she is grateful for having come so far. They will be prayers, a kind of thank-you note.

She was lulled into believing these narratives of change were a necessary accomplishment. What was curious about these attempts was she remembered almost nothing of American history. In her mind the names—*Mayflower*, *Pilgrim*, and *Plymouth Rock*—were associated with businesses; one on a moving van, the other two in insurance ads.

After the War (I)

When Sun Yat-sen was elected President,
he appointed her father Ambassador to Belgium.
There is a photograph of him
dressed like an admiral
from around this time.
The photograph is framed
and stands on a bookcase.
Once, after the glass was broken,
she wrapped it in Saran Wrap.
It has been more than five years
since the glass was swept up,
and she has expressed neither the need
nor the desire to replace it.

After the War (II)

Grimness was the part of the past
continually stalking him.
And on the evenings it cornered him
at the table, drinking beer
and picking at his dinner,
it interrogated him about everything
he was trying to forget
until the same stories emerged
as pieces of glass methodically pulled
from wounds no one could heal
and waved like a sword
over those who were listening.

After the War (III)

When she sailed to America
she met a young Canadian journalist.
Years later he was elected
Prime Minister of Canada.
She realized she knew him
after reading a gossip column
about his wife's extramarital affairs,
and sent him a letter.
He sent back a snapshot
of the family, husband and wife
smiling proudly beside their two children.
She placed it beside a photograph of her father.

After the War (IV)

When survival is your only desire, you
try to reach the future before it arrives.
For some the journey is never completed.
Once, while she was working nights
in a nearby drugstore, he made dinner.
As he was warming up the can of beef stew,
the top of the salt shaker fell off, emptying
the contents into a bubbling pot.
Nothing was said about the mishap.
He sat down and began eating,
quietly finishing everything on his plate.
He expected his son to do the same.

Nantucket

It was late in the afternoon when I returned with the paper bag. I had been cradling it in the crook of my right arm, and steadying it with my left hand, as if the bag contained a plant of some sort. Sweat darkened my shirt and made my forehead glisten, like a car fender in the rain, by the time I slid sideways into the cottage by nudging the screen door with my shoulder. Something either I or the cat started doing last summer.

I realized how light the bag was, only after I put it on the kitchen table and began looking for the scissors. It's an ordinary paper bag with a dark brown stain on one side. Perhaps it once contained some apples, one of which was rotten, or a damp pair of gardener's gloves and a screwdriver. As I knelt beside the only road on this end of the island, a long bright car sped by, and someone's hand let the bag flutter down beside me, as if they knew what I needed then.

How else could I have carried the skeleton home? It was lying on its side beneath a row of raspberry bushes, and looked— because of the seaworthy curve of its bones—like a half-finished model of a whaling ship.

Usually such a ship is placed inside a bottle. I suppose, yes, it is a testament to the craftsmen to be amazed by the number of details they managed to include. Cannon, Captain's table, lamp, and winch: these things should not be taken for granted, though I distinctly felt at that moment that what anyone really wants to find when they look into a bottle is that an essential element has been overlooked. A marred perfection is what the viewers (and I must, for the moment, align myself with them) are after, though not of the kind those craftsmen attained.

It was once a puppy, that much is obvious. There is a white plastic collar around its neck, and not one of the rhinestones is missing. It was the collar that made me want to take it home. It underlined the weight of the bones in a way nothing else could. I knew immediately that they were the perfect memento of this island; this scrap of grass and rock that used to wait for the whaling ships to return; their holds full of oil, and in the pocket of each sailor some scrimshaw.

Broken Off by the Music

With the first gray light of dawn the remnants
of gas stations and supermarkets assume their
former shapes. A freckled, redheaded boy
stares into the refrigerator, its chrome shelves
lined with jars, cans, and bottles—each
appropriately labeled with a word and a picture.
For some of the other inhabitants of the yellow
apartment house, the mere vapor of food
in the morning is sufficient nourishment.

Along the highway dozens of motorists have pulled
onto the shoulder of the road, no longer guided
by the flicker of countless stars dancing over
the surface of asphalt. Three radios
disagree over what lies ahead. It is morning,
and sand no longer trickles onto the austere
boulevards of the capital.

Outside, on the sidewalk, two girls kneel down
and pray in front of a restaurant closed for
vacation. A breeze reminds everyone that ice
is another jewel—the result of snow gleaming
at night. "I used to play on this street,
but now it is different," says the older girl.
The younger one, who might be her sister, nods
solemnly. Across the street is a store
no one will enter.

Distance can hardly lend enchantment to the remnants
of a supermarket where faces are torn, as always,
between necessity and desire. With the first gray
light of evening a freckled girl assumes her former
shape—each limb appropriately labeled with words

of instruction. The younger boy skips away from
the others, while singing a song full of words
he stumbles over.

Outside the capital, two motorists disagree over
the remnants of a refrigerator. Three boys stare
at what lies behind the stars. A breeze reminds
everyone of their former shapes, while evening
lends an austere enchantment to the yellow window
of a gas station.

Snow can hardly lend enchantment to a sidewalk
where two young girls shiver uncontrollably,
while looking for the doorway of a store
that is closed. Nearby, a woman labels
gray shapes with songs of disagreement.

Three supermarkets disagree over the food vapors
in a refrigerator. Along the highway sand
becomes a song of chrome enchantment. A young boy
kicks the remnants of his brother's radio.
"I used to pray on this street, but now it is
sufficient to return each afternoon," he whispers,
as if someone were listening.

A woman stops in front of a gas station and stares
at the surface of the stars drifting through the
clouds. The breeze reminds the motorist that the
first gray light of dawn is the remnant of a jewel.

Thousands of radios begin flickering throughout
the apartment complex.

The shoulders of the younger sister are covered
with snow. The sidewalk in front of the restaurant
is littered with sleeping motorists, each of them

staring at the breeze trickling from the clouds.
But at night, the sky is a window full of earrings,
each lost in its blue velvet box.

Two boys nod solemnly in front of their former shapes.
Someone has embroidered the remnants of sufficient
enchantment.

Two Kinds of Language

1

It was nearly evening when the father returned home from work. At the other end of the city the sun had started cooling, like a ball of molten metal. A reddish glowing light streaked the walls of the living room.

He sat in the room and listened to his parents talking in the language they brought from China. Often he began squirming, trying to understand what was being said amidst the smells and sounds of cooking. Usually they began talking this way when they didn't want him to understand what was being discussed. Sometimes it was him. He couldn't always tell. If he listened hard enough, what he thought he understood was the intonation and the voice, rather than what was being said.

2

They were driving on the back roads through North Carolina. The radio was on, a yellow eye blinking inside the car's concave shell. An electric heart. Neither of them spoke, as song after song filled the car. Occasionally, he changed the station, or offered to light her cigarette. All the songs seemed to tell a similar story, and yet the words and music never quite seemed to fit together.

He sank further into his seat, looked out the window, and listened. Beneath the moon's diligent patrol the fields stretched out to the horizon. Inside the car it felt the same to him as it did before, when he was a child.

In the other room someone was speaking a language he could barely understand.

Shimmering Pediment

An overloaded circuit—lightning
Jammed the horizon, and for days
The echoes remained in my eyes.
But the brightest star is to begin
Anywhere. "Among the peonies,"
As an ancient Chinese poet wrote . . .

Near where the river pirouettes
Past the airplane graveyard
I wandered in as a child;
A fenced-in field; the broken
Fuselages and crumpled wings
Reclining, like sunbathers, in
Haphazard rows of damaged magnificence.

Actually, I never played on this knoll,
Though I think somehow I must have.
For around supper I felt compelled
To return to that silent and empty
Amphitheater, my plane spiraling
In a diminishing circle, as I flew
Parallel to where I am now standing.

Some fish we peel back, leaving only the bones. Others devour us, leaving only the stories. This one begins in a garden in China, where a young prince is sitting alone on a bench beside a turquoise pond. Each time he snaps his fingers and whistles, the golden red sunset of a carp can be seen rising toward the surface. Five fat scavengers rule this manicured kingdom, and each of them has been endowed with the nobility of a name. When the boy leaves the palace at noon and walks across the garden to feed them, the moment is as precise and refined as the emblematic flowers stitched across his robe.

On a warm summer afternoon the algae-covered pond is as green as nights in the Arctic when embedded arrows of light sparkle in the sky. For a few moments the boy watches the clouds stretch like cats across the glassy surface. Soon it will be his sixth birthday, and another carp will join the kingdom.

The clouds turn into dragons and back again. The moon trembles against the sky, a slivered almond. One day melts into another.

In the pond the carp are still listening, unable to hear their names drift over the kingdom. The prince is sick and they have been forgotten. Patiently, they circle through their palace, looking for the entrance to the room where their master lies, his body burning with fever, his face as crimson as an apple, ripe and ready to fall. Above them only the murmur of the wind hurrying through the mulberry branches.

Eventually, the countryside succumbs to disease and terror. Succeeding reigns of tyrants—their names twisting through history like snakes—bury the pond beneath their own inter-pretation of heaven's grandeur. Meanwhile, the carp burrow into a book by someone whose ability to remember facts cir-cumscribes his desire to tell stories.

. . .

To the young boy standing in front of the large glass tanks, each hypnotic with activity, all the goldfish looked more or less the same. It was only after he stared into one tank for a long time that he saw any difference among them. He chose the two smallest, the ones that would have the most trouble surviving were someone to let them go.

When he got home, his father lay on the couch and took a nap. The mother was out visiting a friend. Already the shadows of the narrow street had started filing quietly into the room.

He lay on his stomach on the floor and stared intently at the fish. Back and forth they swam, unconcerned with their intruder. They looked as if the only thought on their minds was escape. It was difficult to name creatures so alien and indifferent, and he had not been able to find any that he liked.

As the fish darted from side to side, the young boy wondered what he could do to make them more comfortable. They must get tired, he thought. And yet they do not seem sleepy. The room was filled with the signs of evening's approach. He lay in the darkness and remembered the way the ocean rocked endlessly the day his parents took him to the beach. Beside him the fish swirled once more in their bowl. Nearby, his father snored.

In the bedroom he found his dump truck beside a pile of soldiers and blocks, and brought it back to the living room. Carefully, so as not to spill any water, he placed the fishbowl on the back of the truck. Then he lay back on the floor and began slowly pushing the truck back and forth. His father stirred slightly and then sank back into sleep.

The boy watched the water sloshing against the sides of the bowl, like the ocean, and was momentarily relieved. He adjusted the speed with which he moved the truck to a slower, more rhythmic pace. Then he realized what they needed besides this comforting motion was salt. He remembered the stinging taste of the waves as they tried to knock him over, his mother beside him so he would not be afraid. One teaspoon, a little more rocking, and they would soon be asleep. His arm was tired, but he continued to push the truck back and forth in the darkened room. He knew he could not stop until they were resting, comfortable in their new home.

NOTES

"Corpse and Mirror" is the title of a painting by Jasper Johns.

"Persons in the Presence of a Metamorphosis" is the title of a painting by Joan Miró.

Etienne-Louis Boullée (1728-1799) was an architect who, in the course of his career, built very little but produced numerous designs. Among his designs was a "Project for a Newton Memorial" in the shape of a giant sphere and a "Project for a Tomb for the Spartans."